MILITARY MACHINES

MILITARY HELICOPTERS

by Melissa Abramovitz

Consulting Editor: Gail Saunders-Smith, PhD

Consultant: Raymond L. Puffer, PhD
Historian, Ret.
Edwards Air Force Base History Office

CAPSTONE PRESS
a capstone imprint

Pebble Plus is published by Capstone Press,
1710 Roe Crest Drive, North Mankato, Minnesota 56003.
www.capstonepub.com

Library of Congress Cataloging-in-Publication Data
Abramovitz, Melissa, 1954–
  Military helicopters / by Melissa Abramovitz.
    p. cm.—(Pebble plus. Military machines)
  Includes bibliographical references and index.
  Summary: "Simple text and full-color photographs describe various military helicopters"—Provided by publisher.
  ISBN 978-1-4296-7574-1 (library binding)
  ISBN 978-1-4296-7883-4 (paperback)
  1. Military helicopters—United States—Juvenile literature. I. Title.
  UG1233.A27 2012
  623.74'6047—dc23   2011021656

Editorial Credits
Erika L. Shores, editor; Kyle Grenz, designer; Kathy McColley, production specialist

Photo Credits
DoD photo by MC3 Casey H. Kyhl, 7
U.S. Air Force photo by Senior Airman Julianne Showalter, 11, Senior Airman Kenny Holston, 15, Staff Sgt. Greg L.
    Davis, 13, Staff Sgt. James L. Harper Jr., 9, 21
U.S. Army photo by Sgt. 1st Class Sadie Bleistein, 19, Spc. Eric Cabral, cover
U.S. Marine Corps photo by Cpl. Richard A. Tetreau, 17, Staff Sgt. Chad L. Simon, 5

Artistic Effects
Shutterstock: Hitdelight

Note to Parents and Teachers

The Military Machines series supports national science standards related to science, technology, and society. This book describes and illustrates military helicopters. The images support early readers in understanding the text. The repetition of words and phrases helps early readers learn new words. This book also introduces early readers to subject-specific vocabulary words, which are defined in the Glossary section. Early readers may need assistance to read some words and to use the Table of Contents, Glossary, Read More, Internet Sites, and Index sections of the book.

Printed in the United States of America in North Mankato, Minnesota.
102011   006405CGS12

Table of Contents

What Are Military Helicopters?

Military helicopters are mighty machines. They fight battles over land and sea. They carry supplies and rescue people.

Helicopters go straight up and down, forward, sideways, and backward. Helicopters don't need runways. They take off and land in small spaces.

Parts of Military Helicopters

Huge spinning rotor blades lift helicopters. Rotors also let helicopters hover. Small tail rotors help helicopters turn.

Some helicopters have
wheels to land on.
Other helicopters land on
metal tubes called skids.

Guns and missiles are mounted on military helicopters. Gunners shoot to defend troops and attack enemy targets.

Helicopters in the Military

Chinook helicopters take troops, weapons, and supplies where the military needs them. Chinooks can carry two trucks and 33 people.

Iroquois helicopters do land
and sea search and rescue.
They bring in rescue crews
and carry hurt troops to hospitals.

Apache Longbow attack helicopters shoot enemy targets with guns, missiles, and rockets. They also spy on enemies.

Military Machines

Military helicopters take supplies and troops wherever they are needed. Helicopters let the U.S. Armed Forces fight battles anywhere in the world.

Glossary

Armed Forces—the whole military; the U.S. Armed Forces include the Army, Navy, Air Force, Marine Corps, and Coast Guard

hover—to remain in one place in the air

missile—a weapon that is fired at or dropped on a target

rescue—to save someone who is in danger

rotor blade—a long narrow wing that spins on top of a helicopter; a rotor blade lifts and controls a helicopter

skid—one of two long metal tubes on which some helicopters land

spy—to find out about enemies in a secret way

Read More

Braulick, Carrie A. *U.S. Army Helicopters*. Military Vehicles. Mankato, Minn.: Capstone Press, 2006.

Doman, Mary Kate. *Big Military Machines*. All about Big Machines. Berkeley Heights, N.J.: Enslow Publishers, 2012.

Ellis, Catherine. *Helicopters*. Mega Military Machines. New York: PowerKids Press, 2007.

Internet Sites

FactHound offers a safe, fun way to find Internet sites related to this book. All of the sites on FactHound have been researched by our staff.

Here's all you do:

Visit *www.facthound.com*

Type in this code: 9781429675741

Check out projects, games and lots more at
www.capstonekids.com

Index

Word Count: 168
Grade: 1
Early-Intervention Level: 22